RANJOT SINGH CHAHAL

7 Steps to Think Positive
Achieve Success Through a Positive Mindset

First published by Rana Books (UK, INDIA) 2023

Copyright © 2023 by Ranjot Singh Chahal

All rights reserved. No part of this publication may be reproduced, stored or transmitted in any form or by any means, electronic, mechanical, photocopying, recording, scanning, or otherwise without written permission from the publisher. It is illegal to copy this book, post it to a website, or distribute it by any other means without permission.

First edition

ISBN: 978-81-19786-30-5

Contents

Step 1: Recognize Negative Thoughts	1
Step 2: Challenge Negative Thoughts	4
Step 3: Reframe Negative Thoughts	9
Step 4: Cultivate Gratitude	13
Step 5: Surround Yourself with Positivity	17
Step 6: Practice Self-Care	22
Step 7: Celebrate Small Victories and Progress	27
Conclusion	31
Tips for Positive Thinking	33
100 ways to enjoy life with Positivity	36
100 Motivational Tips	40

Step 1: Recognize Negative Thoughts

a. Understanding the Impact of Negative Thinking

Negative thinking refers to a pattern of thoughts that are primarily pessimistic self-critical and judgmental. These thoughts focus on dwelling on the negative aspects of situations ourselves or others and can have a detrimental impact on our mental and emotional well-being. Recognizing negative thinking is the first step towards challenging and changing these patterns.

Negative thinking can manifest in various ways and can strongly influence our emotions behavior and overall perception of ourselves and the world around us. When we consistently engage in negative thinking it can contribute to feelings of sadness anxiety and low self-esteem. It can also impact our relationships decision-making abilities and our ability to cope with stress.

For example imagine a person who constantly thinks "I will never be successful." This negative thought pattern can lead to feelings of hopelessness and demotivation which may hinder them from pursuing their goals and finding fulfillment. It can also influence their behavior by causing them to avoid opportunities or take on a defeatist attitude.

b. Identifying Negative Thought Patterns

Identifying negative thought patterns involves bringing conscious awareness to our thoughts and recognizing when they are predominantly negative. Here are a few common negative thought patterns to look out for:

1. All-or-nothing thinking: This is the tendency to think in extreme terms of absolute success or failure with no room for middle ground. For example someone might think "If I don't get a perfect score on the test I'm a complete failure."

2. Overgeneralization: This involves making sweeping conclusions based on limited evidence. For instance after one rejection someone might think "I'll never find a job. No one wants to hire me."

3. Mental filtering: This happens when we focus solely on the negative aspects of a situation while disregarding any positive aspects. Someone who receives a few critical comments on their work despite also receiving praise may only focus on the criticism ignoring the positive feedback they received.

4. Personalization: This involves taking events personally and attributing them to internal factors even when they are due to external factors. For example if a friend cancels plans someone might think "They canceled because they don't like me."

5. Catastrophizing: This is the tendency to anticipate the worst-

STEP 1: RECOGNIZE NEGATIVE THOUGHTS

case scenario and blow things out of proportion. For instance someone might think "If I fail this presentation my career is ruined and I'll never succeed."

Recognizing these patterns can help us become more aware of our negative thinking and its impact on our well-being. It allows us to challenge and reframe these thoughts leading to a more positive and constructive mindset.

Step 2: Challenge Negative Thoughts

Challenging negative thoughts is an important step in cognitive restructuring a therapy technique used to identify and change irrational thoughts. By questioning the validity of negative thoughts seeking alternative perspectives and examining evidence supporting positive outcomes we can effectively challenge and reframe negativity. In this section we will explore these three strategies in-depth providing examples along the way.

a. Questioning the Validity of Negative Thoughts:

When negative thoughts arise it's essential to question their validity. Often our negative thoughts are biased distorted or based on irrational beliefs. By critically examining these thoughts we can challenge their accuracy and significance. Here are some questions you can ask to challenge negative thoughts:

1. Is there evidence to support this thought?
   For example if you're feeling anxious about giving a presentation ask yourself if there is any concrete evidence that suggests

STEP 2: CHALLENGE NEGATIVE THOUGHTS

you will fail. Is it based on past experiences personal beliefs or simply fear?

2. Could there be alternative explanations?

Consider other explanations or interpretations for the negative thought. For instance if you receive criticism at work instead of automatically assuming you're not good enough consider the possibility that your manager might be having a bad day or offering constructive feedback.

3. Am I jumping to conclusions?

Our minds have a tendency to make assumptions based on limited information. If you find yourself making catastrophic predictions or assuming the worst outcome ask if there is any concrete evidence to support these assumptions.

4. Could there be a more balanced perspective?

Negative thoughts often magnify the negative aspects while minimizing the positive. Challenge this bias by identifying positive aspects or potential outcomes that are being overlooked or downplayed. Consider a more balanced viewpoint to counteract the negativity.

By questioning the validity of negative thoughts we can start to break the cycle of negative thinking and see things from a more realistic and rational perspective.

b. Seeking Alternative Perspectives:

Another powerful way to challenge negative thoughts is by seeking alternative perspectives. Negative thoughts often stem from rigid thinking patterns and a narrow view of situations. By considering different viewpoints we can broaden our understanding and challenge our automatic negative thoughts. Here are some strategies to seek alternative perspectives:

1. Put yourself in someone else's shoes:

Imagine how a trusted friend or family member would interpret the situation. This exercise can help you gain a different perspective and break free from your negative mindset.

2. Seek feedback from others:

Reach out to someone you trust and ask for their opinion on the situation. By getting an outside perspective you may gain insights that you hadn't considered before.

3. Challenge your own biases:

Recognize if your negative thoughts are influenced by preconceived notions or personal biases. Be open to the possibility that your perspective may not be entirely accurate or fair.

4. Engage in active listening:

When interacting with others practice active listening. Pay attention to their words tone and body language and try to understand their viewpoint without judgment. This exercise can help you challenge your own assumptions and broaden your perspective.

By seeking alternative perspectives we can challenge the negative thoughts that often result from distorted thinking patterns and gain a more balanced view of the situation.

STEP 2: CHALLENGE NEGATIVE THOUGHTS

c. Examining Evidence Supporting Positive Outcomes:

Examining the evidence supporting positive outcomes is a technique that helps counteract negative thoughts by focusing on realistic possibilities and positive aspects. By consciously acknowledging the evidence supporting positive outcomes we can challenge the overwhelming negativity that often accompanies negative thoughts. Here are some strategies to examine evidence supporting positive outcomes:

1. Identify past successes:
Recall previous situations where you have successfully managed challenges or achieved your goals. Remind yourself of the skills strengths and strategies that helped you succeed.

2. Gather evidence of positive moments:
Pay attention to the positive experiences compliments or achievements no matter how small they may seem. Documenting them in a journal or gratitude journal can serve as a valuable reminder of positive aspects in your life.

3. Consider alternative outcomes:
Instead of solely focusing on worst-case scenarios consciously consider other possible outcomes. Deliberately generate alternative positive outcomes and entertain the idea that they could happen too.

4. Develop a positive mindset:
Cultivate a positive mindset by practicing positive affirmations gratitude and mindfulness. These techniques can help shift your attention towards the positive aspects of life fostering

a more optimistic outlook.

Examining the evidence supporting positive outcomes helps counteract the confirmation bias where we selectively focus on evidence that supports our negative thoughts while ignoring or discounting positive aspects. By consciously acknowledging positive evidence we bring balance to our thinking patterns and allow for the possibility of positive outcomes.

In conclusion challenging negative thoughts is a crucial step in cognitive restructuring. By questioning the validity of negative thoughts seeking alternative perspectives and examining evidence supporting positive outcomes we can effectively challenge and reframe negativity. These strategies help us break free from distorted thinking patterns gain a more balanced perspective and foster a positive mindset. With practice we can develop a more realistic and optimistic outlook leading to improved emotional well-being and a more fulfilling life.

Step 3: Reframe Negative Thoughts

a. Shifting the Focus to Positive Aspects:

One effective way to reframe negative thoughts is to shift our focus to positive aspects. This involves consciously choosing to look at the brighter side of things and finding the good in a situation. By doing so we can alter our perspective and enhance our overall well-being.

For example let's say you didn't get the promotion you were hoping for at work. Instead of dwelling on the negative aspects shift your focus to the positive aspects. Perhaps this setback can be an opportunity for personal growth and skill development. You can utilize this time to improve your skills seek new opportunities or explore other career options that align with your goals and interests.

Similarly in challenging situations such as facing a difficult breakup focusing on the positive aspects can help you navigate through the process. Instead of getting consumed by negative thoughts and emotions you can reframe your perspective by acknowledging the valuable life lessons learned personal growth achieved and newfound opportunities for self-discovery and self-care.

By deliberately shifting our focus to positive aspects we can decrease negative thinking patterns reduce stress levels and foster a more optimistic mindset.

b. Finding Silver Linings in Challenging Situations:

Finding silver linings in challenging situations involves actively seeking positive or valuable aspects even in the midst of adversity. It allows us to find hope resilience and meaning in difficult times.

For instance let's consider a scenario where you unexpectedly lose your job. Instead of dwelling on the negative aspects finding a silver lining could involve recognizing this as an opportunity for a career change or pursuing a long-withheld dream. You may find that being forced out of your comfort zone can lead to personal and professional growth new friendships or even more time to devote to passions and hobbies.

Similarly during a global pandemic like COVID-19 finding silver linings could involve appreciating the extra time spent with family the chance to learn new skills or hobbies or the reevaluation of one's priorities and values. It's not about denying the challenges and hardships but rather finding the positives within them.

By actively seeking silver linings in challenging situations we can cultivate resilience maintain a hopeful outlook and adapt to difficult circumstances with greater ease.

STEP 3: REFRAME NEGATIVE THOUGHTS

c. Using Affirmations and Positive Self-talk:

Affirmations and positive self-talk are powerful tools that can help reframe negative thoughts and promote a more positive and empowering mindset. Affirmations are positive statements that we repeat to ourselves to reinforce positive beliefs or intentions. Positive self-talk involves replacing negative self-talk with uplifting supportive and encouraging internal dialogue.

For example if you find yourself often having negative thoughts about your abilities you can use affirmations such as "I am capable and resourceful. I can handle any challenge that comes my way." Repeating these affirmations regularly can reshape your self-perception and boost your confidence.

Positive self-talk can be useful in challenging situations as well. Instead of criticizing yourself or assuming the worst you can consciously choose to encourage and support yourself. For instance if you make a mistake at work rather than bashing yourself you can say "It's okay mistakes happen. I will learn from this experience and do better next time."

By consistently using affirmations and practicing positive self-talk we can rewire our thought patterns develop a more compassionate inner voice and foster a resilient and optimistic mindset.

Conclusion:

Reframing negative thoughts is a powerful skill that can enhance our overall well-being. By shifting our focus to positive aspects finding silver linings in challenging situations and employing affirmations and positive self-talk we can reframe our perspective and cultivate a more positive and empowering mindset.

Remember it takes practice and consistent effort to reframe negative thoughts effectively. Be patient with yourself and celebrate small victories along the way. Over time you'll find that reframing negative thoughts becomes easier and you'll experience the numerous benefits it brings to your mental and emotional well-being.

Step 4: Cultivate Gratitude

In this step we will explore ways to cultivate gratitude in our lives. Gratitude is the practice of recognizing and appreciating the good things that we have in our lives. It is a powerful tool for increasing our happiness improving our relationships and overall well-being. In this section we will discuss three specific practices that can help us cultivate gratitude: practicing gratitude daily keeping a gratitude journal and expressing gratitude to others.

a. Practicing Gratitude Daily

One of the most effective ways to cultivate gratitude is by making it a daily practice. By intentionally focusing on the things we are grateful for each day we can shift our attention away from negative thoughts and towards the positive aspects of our lives. This practice helps us develop a more positive outlook and increases our overall sense of well-being.

There are various ways to incorporate daily gratitude into our lives. One simple practice is to start each day by mentally listing three things we are grateful for. These can be big or small ranging from our health and loved ones to a beautiful sunrise or a kind gesture from a stranger. This exercise helps us shift our mindset to focus on the positive aspects of our lives right from the start of the day.

Another powerful practice is to practice gratitude throughout the day by taking moments to pause and appreciate the good things as they occur. This can be as simple as savoring a delicious meal noticing the beauty of nature or expressing gratitude for the kindness of a friend or colleague. By consciously acknowledging and appreciating these moments we can enhance our overall sense of gratitude.

b. Keeping a Gratitude Journal

Keeping a gratitude journal is another effective way to cultivate gratitude. This practice involves taking a few minutes each day to write down the things we are grateful for. By putting our thoughts into writing we enhance our ability to truly reflect on and appreciate these things.

To start a gratitude journal find a notebook or journal dedicated solely to this practice. Set aside a few minutes each day to write down three to five things you are grateful for. Try to be specific and descriptive in your entries focusing on the details that make these things special.

For example instead of simply writing "I'm grateful for my family you could write "I'm grateful for my family because they provide me with love support and laughter. Their presence in my life brings me joy and helps me navigate challenges."

By regularly engaging in this practice you will start to notice patterns and themes of gratitude in your life. You may also discover that as you actively look for things to be grateful for your ability to find and appreciate them increases. Over time this can lead to a more positive and grateful mindset.

c. Expressing Gratitude to Others

Expressing gratitude to others is a powerful way to cultivate gratitude not only in ourselves but also in our relationships. By acknowledging and appreciating the efforts and kindness of others we strengthen our connections and create a more positive and harmonious environment.

There are many ways to express gratitude to others. One simple yet meaningful practice is to verbalize our appreciation. Take the time to tell someone how much you appreciate their support kindness or any positive impact they have had on your life. This can be a simple thank-you note an in-person conversation or even a phone call expressing your gratitude.

Another way to express gratitude is through acts of kindness. When someone does something for you whether big or small take the time to show your gratitude by reciprocating or doing something thoughtful in return. This not only shows appreciation but also reinforces a cycle of gratitude and kindness.

Additionally writing and sending gratitude letters can be a powerful way to express our appreciation. Take the time to write a heartfelt letter to someone who has made a positive impact on your life expressing your gratitude and highlighting specific reasons for your appreciation. This act not only cultivates gratitude in ourselves but also brings joy and happiness to the recipient.

By practicing gratitude daily keeping a gratitude journal and expressing gratitude to others we can develop a more grateful mindset and enhance our overall well-being. These practices help us shift our focus towards the positive aspects of our lives foster stronger relationships and create a more positive and harmonious environment.

Gratitude is a habit that can be nurtured and cultivated with regular practice. As we develop a deeper sense of gratitude we become more resilient in the face of challenges more appreciative of the present moment and more content with our lives. So let us start incorporating these practices into our daily lives and experience the transformative power of gratitude.

Step 5: Surround Yourself with Positivity

In our journey towards personal growth and happiness the people we surround ourselves with and the activities we engage in play a crucial role. Surrounding ourselves with positivity can have a powerful impact on our mindset emotions and overall well-being. In this step we will explore the importance of choosing supportive and positive individuals engaging in activities that uplift and inspire us and avoiding negative influences.

a. Choosing Supportive and Positive Individuals:

The people we choose to spend our time with can significantly affect our outlook on life self-esteem and overall happiness. It is essential to surround ourselves with individuals who genuinely care about our well-being support our goals and uplift us. These individuals can include friends family members mentors or even online communities.

Supportive individuals provide encouragement motivation and a sense of belonging. They celebrate our successes stand by us in times of difficulty and provide a positive influence on our lives. When we are surrounded by people who believe in us and our dreams it becomes easier to maintain a positive mindset and overcome obstacles.

On the other hand negative and unsupportive individuals can drain our energy instill self-doubt and hold us back from reaching our full potential. These individuals may constantly criticize belittle or discourage us. Identifying such toxic relationships is crucial for our personal growth. It may be necessary to create some distance or even sever ties with individuals who consistently undermine our positivity and progress.

Example:

Consider a scenario where you aspire to start your own business. Surrounding yourself with positive and supportive individuals who have experience in entrepreneurship can be incredibly beneficial. These individuals can offer valuable insights provide guidance and even collaborate on projects. They may serve as a source of inspiration and motivation pushing you to pursue your dreams. On the other hand if you were surrounded by negative individuals who constantly doubted your abilities or discouraged you from taking risks it would be challenging to maintain a positive mindset and move forward with your business goals.

b. Engaging in Activities that Uplift and Inspire:

In addition to the people we surround ourselves with the activities we engage in also impact our overall well-being.

STEP 5: SURROUND YOURSELF WITH POSITIVITY

Engaging in activities that uplift and inspire us can fuel our motivation boost our mood and help us maintain a positive outlook on life.

Uplifting activities can take various forms depending on our interests and preferences. Some examples include:

1. Pursuing hobbies: Engaging in activities we enjoy such as painting playing an instrument gardening or cooking can bring joy and fulfillment to our lives. These activities allow us to express ourselves creatively and engage in something that brings us genuine satisfaction.

2. Physical exercise: Engaging in regular physical exercise whether it be through sports yoga dancing or going for regular walks has numerous benefits for our physical and mental well-being. Exercise releases endorphins which are known as the "feel-good" hormones boosting our mood and reducing stress.

3. Seeking knowledge: Engaging in activities that expand our knowledge and stimulate our minds can be highly inspiring. This can include reading books attending seminars or workshops listening to podcasts or taking up online courses. Continuous learning helps us grow intellectually and keeps our minds sharp.

4. Spending time in nature: Connecting with nature has a calming and rejuvenating effect on our well-being. Whether it's going for a hike spending time at the beach or simply sitting in a park immersing ourselves in nature can bring a sense of peace and serenity.

By consciously incorporating uplifting activities into our daily lives we create an environment that nurtures positivity and inspiration. These activities can serve as a form of self-care allowing us to recharge and maintain a healthy mindset.

Example:

Let's say you find solace in writing. Setting aside time each day to write in a journal or work on a creative writing project can be a deeply uplifting and inspiring activity for you. It allows you to express yourself process your thoughts and emotions and tap into your creativity. Engaging in this activity regularly acts as a source of positivity enabling you to maintain a positive mindset and nurture your personal growth.

c. Avoiding Negative Influences:

Apart from surrounding ourselves with positive individuals and engaging in uplifting activities it is equally important to be mindful of negative influences in our lives. Negative influences can come from various sources including media social media news or even certain environments we find ourselves in.

Media and social media in particular can have a significant impact on our mindset. Constant exposure to negative news comparison with others or toxic online interactions can breed negativity and affect our self-esteem. Being aware of the impact of these influences on our mental well-being is essential. It may be necessary to limit our media consumption or curate our social media feeds to include positive and inspiring content.

Similarly certain environments can be inherently negative and drain our positivity. It might be necessary to assess our surroundings and make necessary changes if we find ourselves in toxic workplaces unhealthy relationships or environments that do not support our personal growth. Surrounding ourselves with positivity also means actively choosing environments that foster our well-being and personal development.

Example:

Imagine you are trying to cultivate positive self-esteem and body image. However you frequently find yourself surrounded by individuals who constantly criticize their own appearance and engage in fat-shaming conversations. These negative influences can significantly affect your own perception of yourself and undermine your efforts towards self-acceptance. Recognizing the negative impact of such environments and consciously seeking out individuals or spaces that promote body positivity and self-love is crucial for maintaining a positive mindset and nurturing personal growth.

In conclusion surrounding ourselves with positivity is an essential step in our journey towards personal growth and happiness. Choosing supportive and positive individuals engaging in activities that uplift and inspire and avoiding negative influences all contribute to creating an environment that fosters our well-being. By intentionally surrounding ourselves with positivity we gain the support motivation and inspiration needed to maintain a positive mindset and cultivate personal growth.

Step 6: Practice Self-Care

Self-care is an essential component of maintaining a healthy lifestyle and overall well-being. It involves taking deliberate actions to nurture and care for oneself both physically and mentally. In today's fast-paced world it is easy to neglect self-care in favor of other responsibilities. However neglecting self-care can lead to burnout increased stress levels and a decrease in overall happiness and satisfaction.

In this step we will explore three important aspects of self-care: taking time for rest and relaxation engaging in activities you enjoy and prioritizing physical and mental well-being. Each of these components contributes to an individual's overall self-care routine and plays a crucial role in maintaining balance and well-being.

a. Taking Time for Rest and Relaxation

Rest and relaxation are essential for recharging and replenishing the mind and body. It is crucial to carve out designated time for rest and relaxation in your daily or weekly schedule. Whether it's a few minutes of meditation a long bath or simply sitting in silence taking time to relax can reduce stress and promote a sense of calm.

One effective method of relaxation is deep breathing exercises. These exercises involve slow deep breaths that help relax the body and calm the mind. For example you can try diaphragmatic breathing by inhaling deeply through your nose allowing your abdomen to rise. Hold your breath for a few seconds then exhale slowly through your mouth allowing your abdomen to fall. Repeat this process several times focusing on the rhythm of your breath.

Another technique for rest and relaxation is progressive muscle relaxation. This technique involves tensing and then relaxing different muscle groups in the body promoting a sense of physical and mental relaxation. Start by tensing your muscles for a few seconds then release the tension and notice the difference in sensation. Move through different muscle groups such as your hands arms shoulders and so on until you feel relaxed and rejuvenated.

b. Engaging in Activities You Enjoy

Engaging in activities you enjoy is another critical aspect of self-care. It allows you to reconnect with yourself find joy and fulfillment and maintain your mental and emotional well-being. These activities can vary greatly from person to person based on individual preferences and interests.

For example some people find solace in creative pursuits such as painting playing a musical instrument or writing. Engaging in these activities not only provides an outlet for self-expression but also promotes relaxation and stress relief. Others may find enjoyment and relaxation in physical activities like hiking dancing or yoga. These activities not only provide opportunities for exercise but also release endorphins which boost mood and overall well-being.

Engaging in activities you enjoy can also involve social interactions. Spending time with loved ones whether it's a family member friend or even a pet can provide a sense of connection and support. Engaging in conversations engaging in shared interests or simply spending quality time together can have a positive impact on your emotional well-being.

c. Prioritizing Physical and Mental Well-being

One of the fundamental aspects of self-care is prioritizing both physical and mental well-being. This involves paying attention to your physical health such as exercise nutrition and sleep as well as nurturing your mental health through practices like mindfulness and positive self-talk.

Regular physical exercise is crucial for maintaining physical health and overall well-being. It improves cardiovascular health strengthens muscles and bones and releases endorphins which can elevate mood. Whether it's a brisk walk a jog or a workout routine at the gym finding an activity you enjoy and incorporating it into your routine can significantly impact your physical well-being.

Proper nutrition is equally important for maintaining physical well-being. A balanced diet that includes a variety of fruits vegetables whole grains lean protein and healthy fats provides essential nutrients for optimal bodily function. By prioritizing healthy eating habits and incorporating nutritious meals into your daily routine you can fuel your body and optimize your overall well-being.

Furthermore mental well-being is closely tied to self-care. Practicing mindfulness for instance involves being fully present and aware of the current moment without judgment. This practice allows you to cultivate a sense of focus and calm amidst the busyness of life. You can incorporate mindfulness into your daily routine by engaging in activities such as meditation journaling or mindful walking.

In addition to mindfulness positive self-talk plays a significant role in mental well-being. It involves replacing negative self-talk with positive and empowering statements. by reframing negative thoughts into constructive and supportive narratives you can boost your self-esteem reduce stress and promote a more positive outlook on life.

Conclusion

Practicing self-care is crucial for maintaining a healthy and balanced life. Taking time for rest and relaxation engaging in activities you enjoy and prioritizing physical and mental well-being are essential components of a self-care routine. By incorporating these practices into your daily or weekly routine you can nurture and care for yourself leading to improved well-being reduced stress levels and a greater sense of happiness and satisfaction. Remember self-care is not selfish; it is a necessary investment in yourself.

Step 7: Celebrate Small Victories and Progress

In our journey towards achieving our goals it is essential to celebrate the small victories and acknowledge the progress we make along the way. Celebrating these milestones not only brings a sense of accomplishment but also boosts motivation and helps us stay committed to our goals. In this step we will discuss the importance of acknowledging and appreciating achievements and how to reward ourselves for positive steps taken.

a. Acknowledging and Appreciating Achievements

When working towards our goals it is common to set big long-term objectives. While these goals are important they can often feel overwhelming and distant. To combat this it is crucial to break them down into smaller more manageable tasks. By doing so we create multiple points of achievement along the way.

Acknowledging and appreciating these small victories helps us stay motivated and builds our confidence. Celebrating these milestones allows us to see the progress we have made no matter how small and reinforces our belief in our ability to reach our end goal.

Here are a few ways to acknowledge and appreciate achievements:

1. Reflect and journal: Take the time to reflect on your progress and write it down. Documenting your achievements helps you recognize how far you've come and provides a valuable source of motivation when faced with obstacles.

2. Share your successes: Celebrate your victories with others. Share them with a close friend family member or colleague who can celebrate with you. Their support and encouragement will further reinforce your achievements.

3. Use visual reminders: Create a vision board or use sticky notes with positive affirmations. These visual reminders serve as constant reminders of your achievements and can help you stay focused and motivated.

4. Practice self-compassion: Be kind to yourself and acknowledge that progress is a journey. It's natural to face setbacks and challenges along the way. Instead of beating yourself up over mistakes learn from them and continue pushing forward.

b. Rewarding Yourself for Positive Steps Taken

Rewards play a crucial role in reinforcing positive behavior and motivating us to continue progressing towards our goals. When we reward ourselves we create positive associations with

STEP 7: CELEBRATE SMALL VICTORIES AND PROGRESS

the actions we took to achieve the desired outcome. This helps solidify our commitment to the task at hand and increases the likelihood of repeating those behaviors in the future.

When choosing how to reward yourself it's important to consider what brings you genuine joy and serves as a meaningful reinforcement. Here are some examples of how you can reward yourself for positive steps taken:

1. Treat yourself: Indulge in something you enjoy whether it's going out for a nice dinner buying a new book or pampering yourself with a spa day. These treats serve as tangible rewards that you can look forward to after accomplishing a specific milestone.

2. Take a break: Give yourself permission to take a break and recharge. Whether it's a short vacation a designated rest day or simply spending quality time with loved ones these breaks can provide much-needed relaxation and rejuvenation.

3. Celebrate with others: Invite your friends or loved ones to celebrate your achievements. Plan a gathering or outing to share your success and enjoy the company of those who are important to you. Their presence and support can make the celebration more meaningful and memorable.

4. Personal milestones and rewards system: Set up a personal rewards system for achieving specific milestones. Define these milestones and create a reward that aligns with your values and motivates you. For example if you've successfully completed a challenging project at work treat yourself to a special meal at

your favorite restaurant.

5. Celebrate internally: Not all celebrations have to be external. Sometimes taking a moment to reflect on your achievement and feeling proud of yourself internally can be just as rewarding. Simply acknowledging your hard work and growth can provide a great sense of satisfaction and fulfillment.

Remember the key to effective rewards is to ensure they are meaningful and aligned with your goals and values. They should serve as a positive reinforcement that strengthens your commitment and motivation to continue progressing towards your ultimate objectives.

In conclusion celebrating small victories and acknowledging progress is a vital part of goal achievement. By appreciating these milestones and rewarding ourselves we cultivate a positive mindset boost our motivation and reinforce our commitment to our goals. So take the time to acknowledge your achievements share them with others and don't forget to reward yourself for the positive steps you take on your journey towards success.

Conclusion

Embracing a positive mindset is the key to living a better life. It has a profound impact on our overall well-being, relationships, and success. Here are some key takeaways to conclude the importance of cultivating a positive mindset:

1. **Improved Mental Health**: A positive mindset can help reduce stress, anxiety, and depression. When you focus on the bright side of life, you build resilience and better cope with challenges.
2. **Enhanced Physical Health**: Studies have shown that a positive outlook on life can lead to better physical health. It boosts the immune system, lowers blood pressure, and promotes longevity.
3. **Better Relationships**: Positivity fosters healthier and more fulfilling relationships. When you radiate positivity, you attract like-minded individuals and build stronger connections with others.
4. **Increased Productivity**: A positive mindset fuels motivation and creativity. It encourages you to set and achieve goals, leading to greater personal and professional success.
5. **Resilience in Adversity**: Life is filled with ups and downs. A positive mindset equips you with the resilience

to bounce back from setbacks and turn challenges into opportunities for growth.

6. **Happiness and Fulfillment**: Ultimately, a positive mindset leads to greater happiness and a sense of fulfillment. It allows you to appreciate the present moment and find joy in life's simple pleasures.
7. **Self-Improvement**: Embracing positivity also means embracing personal growth. It encourages a mindset of continuous learning and self-improvement, leading to a more meaningful and purposeful life.

To cultivate a positive mindset, it's essential to practice gratitude, maintain a hopeful outlook, surround yourself with positive influences, and engage in activities that bring you joy. Remember that positivity is a choice you can make every day, and by doing so, you can transform your life for the better. So, let's embrace a positive mindset and unlock the door to a brighter, more fulfilling future.

Tips for Positive Thinking

1. Practice gratitude by consciously appreciating the things you have.
2. Surround yourself with positive and uplifting people.
3. Focus on the present moment instead of dwelling on the past or worrying about the future.
4. Engage in regular exercise as it releases endorphins that can boost your mood.
5. Set realistic goals for yourself and celebrate even the smallest accomplishments.
6. Use positive affirmations to reframe negative thoughts and beliefs.
7. Engage in activities that bring you joy whether it's painting dancing or playing an instrument.
8. Seek out humor and laughter as it can instantly uplift your mood.
9. Practice self-care by prioritizing your mental physical and emotional well-being.
10. Learn to let go of things you cannot control and focus on what you can change.
11. Surround yourself with positive and inspirational quotes or messages.
12. Spend time in nature to reconnect with the beauty around you and promote a sense of peace.
13. Engage in acts of kindness towards others as it can create

a positive ripple effect.

14. Maintain a healthy work-life balance to reduce stress and increase overall positivity.

15. Challenge negative thoughts by replacing them with empowering and constructive ones.

16. Practice deep breathing and relaxation techniques to calm your mind and body.

17. Keep a journal to reflect on positive experiences and capture moments of gratitude.

18. Seek out inspiring books movies or podcasts that promote positivity and personal growth.

19. Volunteer your time or skills to help others which can give you a sense of purpose and fulfillment.

20. Surround yourself with uplifting music that inspires positive emotions.

21. Practice forgiveness both towards others and yourself to release negative energy and find inner peace.

22. Avoid negative news or social media that can drain your energy and focus on uplifting content instead.

23. Nurture and maintain healthy relationships that uplift and support you.

24. Practice mindfulness by being fully present in each moment and appreciating the beauty of the now.

25. Take time for yourself to recharge and engage in activities that bring you joy and relaxation.

26. Celebrate your strengths and achievements no matter how small.

27. Learn from past mistakes and use them as stepping stones for personal growth.

28. Surround yourself with positive and inspirational quotes or messages.

29. Practice visualization and imagine a positive outcome in whatever you set out to do.

30. Engage in acts of random kindness to bring joy to others and create a positive atmosphere.

31. Learn from challenges and setbacks viewing them as opportunities for growth and learning.

32. Practice self-compassion and treat yourself with kindness and understanding.

33. Engage in positive self-talk reminding yourself of your worth and potential.

34. Take breaks and engage in activities that bring you relaxation and joy.

35. Remember that positivity is a mindset that can be cultivated with practice patience and self-awareness.

100 ways to enjoy life with Positivity

1. Wake up with a smile.
2. Practice gratitude daily.
3. Surround yourself with uplifting people.
4. Spend time in nature.
5. Take long walks.
6. Listen to your favorite music.
7. Dance like no one's watching.
8. Try a new hobby.
9. Read inspirational books.
10. Meditate regularly.
11. Volunteer your time.
12. Random acts of kindness.
13. Practice deep breathing.
14. Learn to forgive.
15. Set meaningful goals.
16. Celebrate your achievements.
17. Travel and explore new places.
18. Try new foods and cuisines.
19. Express love and appreciation.
20. Keep a journal.
21. Laugh often.
22. Watch funny movies or shows.

23. Practice mindfulness.
24. Connect with old friends.
25. Learn a new language.
26. Exercise regularly.
27. Enjoy a hot bath.
28. Create a vision board.
29. Pamper yourself with self-care.
30. Practice positive affirmations.
31. Take up a creative hobby like painting or writing.
32. Declutter your living space.
33. Focus on the present moment.
34. Learn to say "no" when necessary.
35. Take breaks from technology.
36. Plan a surprise for someone you love.
37. Attend live performances.
38. Keep a bucket list.
39. Express your creativity.
40. Practice yoga.
41. Watch a sunrise or sunset.
42. Learn a musical instrument.
43. Cook a special meal.
44. Host a gathering with friends.
45. Learn from your mistakes.
46. Try a new fitness class.
47. Explore your local community.
48. Practice positive self-talk.
49. Embrace change.
50. Engage in acts of self-compassion.
51. Find beauty in everyday things.
52. Take a digital detox weekend.
53. Set boundaries in your relationships.

54. Focus on your strengths.
55. Keep a gratitude jar.
56. Plant a garden.
57. Learn to let go of grudges.
58. Take up photography.
59. Have a picnic.
60. Send handwritten letters.
61. Start a DIY project.
62. Try a new hairstyle.
63. Practice the "one in, one out" rule for possessions.
64. Learn to play a new sport.
65. Make a list of your favorite quotes.
66. Attend a motivational seminar.
67. Explore your spiritual side.
68. Practice random acts of kindness.
69. Write a letter to your future self.
70. Watch inspiring TED Talks.
71. Join a club or group with shared interests.
72. Go stargazing.
73. Have a spa day at home.
74. Visit an art museum.
75. Take a scenic drive.
76. Attend a comedy show.
77. Learn to cook a new cuisine.
78. Start a podcast or vlog.
79. Organize a themed party.
80. Go camping.
81. Learn to sew or knit.
82. Create a scrapbook of your memories.
83. Have a "no-complaint" day.
84. Practice mindful eating.

85. Try a new type of meditation.
86. Explore your ancestry.
87. Host a game night.
88. Learn about a new culture.
89. Try aromatherapy.
90. Set aside time for hobbies.
91. Take a hot air balloon ride.
92. Keep a jar of your favorite scents.
93. Explore your artistic side through crafts.
94. Start a small business or side hustle.
95. Plan a weekend getaway.
96. Attend a local festival.
97. Join a sports league.
98. Write a letter of appreciation to someone.
99. Practice positive body image.
100. Love yourself unconditionally.

100 Motivational Tips

1. Start each day with gratitude.
2. Believe in your abilities.
3. Set clear, achievable goals.
4. Embrace challenges as opportunities.
5. Learn from your mistakes.
6. Surround yourself with positive people.
7. Practice mindfulness daily.
8. Stay focused on the present moment.
9. Visualize your success.
10. Take small steps toward your goals.
11. Celebrate your progress.
12. Stay persistent in the face of setbacks.
13. Find inspiration in nature.
14. Cultivate a growth mindset.
15. Keep a journal of your achievements.
16. Practice self-compassion.
17. Use positive affirmations.
18. Seek out mentors and role models.
19. Break big goals into smaller tasks.
20. Stay open to new experiences.
21. Trust the timing of your life.
22. Challenge your comfort zone.

23. Prioritize self-care.
24. Believe that you deserve happiness.
25. Learn to say "no" when necessary.
26. Focus on solutions, not problems.
27. Let go of past regrets.
28. Create a vision board.
29. Take responsibility for your actions.
30. Be kind to yourself and others.
31. Face your fears head-on.
32. Practice active listening.
33. Find meaning in your work.
34. Help others whenever you can.
35. Stay persistent in pursuing your dreams.
36. Stay true to your values.
37. Practice forgiveness.
38. Seek out positive role models.
39. Stay curious and keep learning.
40. Stay organized and declutter.
41. Build a strong support system.
42. Maintain a healthy work-life balance.
43. Focus on your strengths.
44. Let go of grudges.
45. Be adaptable and embrace change.
46. Set boundaries in relationships.
47. Find joy in the little things.
48. Keep a gratitude journal.
49. Stay physically active.
50. Develop a morning routine.
51. Stay resilient in the face of adversity.
52. Practice patience.
53. Believe in the power of perseverance.

54. Face challenges with a positive attitude.
55. Treat failure as a stepping stone to success.
56. Seek inspiration from books and quotes.
57. Maintain a sense of humor.
58. Express your creativity.
59. Take breaks to recharge.
60. Focus on self-improvement.
61. Celebrate your uniqueness.
62. Be open to feedback.
63. Live in alignment with your values.
64. Find beauty in diversity.
65. Let go of negative self-talk.
66. Foster a sense of community.
67. Live authentically.
68. Practice deep breathing exercises.
69. Stay committed to your goals.
70. Believe in the power of love.
71. Develop a positive daily routine.
72. Express gratitude to others.
73. Be a source of positivity for those around you.
74. Embrace uncertainty as an adventure.
75. Cultivate a sense of wonder.
76. Stay resilient in the face of criticism.
77. Surround yourself with supportive friends.
78. Keep a "joy" list of things that make you happy.
79. Stay open to new perspectives.
80. Find purpose in your life.
81. Learn to forgive yourself.
82. Focus on what you can control.
83. Be proactive in problem-solving.
84. Take time to relax and unwind.

85. Express your thoughts and feelings.
86. Let go of perfectionism.
87. Face challenges with courage.
88. Believe that setbacks are temporary.
89. Keep a "victory" jar of your accomplishments.
90. Cultivate a sense of gratitude for the past.
91. Prioritize sleep and rest.
92. Be mindful of your self-talk.
93. Practice random acts of kindness.
94. Cultivate a positive body image.
95. Be a source of encouragement.
96. Set aside time for reflection.
97. Stay committed to personal growth.
98. Believe in your potential.
99. Keep a positive attitude toward aging.
100. Live each day with intention and purpose.

www.ingramcontent.com/pod-product-compliance
Lightning Source LLC
LaVergne TN
LVHW020444080526
838202LV00055B/5334